A GIFT FOR

....

FROM

....

This edition published in 2010 by Hallmark Books,
under license from Thomas Nelson, Inc.
Copyright © 1991 by H. Jackson Brown, Jr.

Life's Little Instruction Book is a registered trademark of
H. Jackson Brown, Jr.

Hallmark Cards, Inc.,
Kansas City, MO 64141
Visit us on the Web at www.Hallmark.com.

Designed by Myra Colbert Advertising & Design

ISBN: 978-1-59530-259-5

BOK1143

Printed and bound in China
OCT09

Life's Little
Instruction Book

511 suggestions, observations,
and reminders on how to live
a happy and rewarding life

BY H. JACKSON BROWN, JR.

THOMAS NELSON PUBLISHERS
Since 1798

GIFT BOOKS
from Hallmark

Introduction

This book began as a gift to my son, Adam. As he packed his stereo, typewriter, blue blazer, and other necessities for his new life as a college freshman, I retreated to the family room to jot down a few observations and words of counsel I thought he might find useful.

I read years ago that it was not the responsibility of parents to pave the road for their children, but to provide a road map. That's how I hoped he would use these mind and heart reflections.

I started writing, and what I thought would take a few hours took several days. I gathered my collection of handwritten notes, typed them up, and put them in a dime-store binder. I walked to the garage and slid it under the front seat of the station wagon.

A few days later his mother and I helped him move into his new dorm room. When he was all settled in, I asked him to come with me to the parking lot. It was time for the presentation. I reached under the car seat and with words to the effect that this was what I knew about living a happy and rewarding life, handed him the bound pages. He hugged me and shook my hand. It was a very special moment.

Well, somehow those typewritten pages became the little book you're now holding. You may not agree with all the entries, and from your own life experience, I'm sure you could add hundreds more. Obviously, some are more important than others, but all have added a degree of joy, meaning, and efficiency to my life.

A few days after I had given Adam his copy, he called me from his dorm room. "Dad," he said, "I've been reading the instruction book and I think it's one of the best gifts I've ever received. I'm going to add to it and someday give it to my son."

Every once in a while life hands you a moment so precious, so overwheiming you almost glow. I know. I had just experienced one.

For Adam, my son and in many ways my teacher.

Son, how can I help you see?
May I give you my shoulders to stand on?
Now you see farther than me.
Now you see for both of us.
Won't you tell me what you see?

1.

Compliment three people every day.

2.

Have a dog.

3.

Watch a sunrise at least once a year.

4.

Remember other people's birthdays.

5.

Overtip breakfast waitresses.

6.

Have a firm handshake.

7.

Look people in the eye.

8.

Say "thank you" a lot.

9.

Say "please" a lot.

10.

Learn to play a musical instrument.

11. Sing in the shower.

12.

Use the good silver.

13.

Learn to make great chili.

14.

Plant flowers every spring.

15.

Own a great stereo system.

16.

Be the first to say, "Hello."

17.

Live beneath your means.

18.

Drive inexpensive cars, but own
the best house you can afford.

19.

Buy great books even if you never read them.

20.

Be forgiving of yourself and others.

21.

Learn three clean jokes.

22.
Wear polished shoes.

23.
Floss your teeth.

24.
Drink champagne for no reason at all.

25.
Ask for a raise when you feel you've earned it.

26.
If in a fight, hit first and hit hard.

27.

Return all things you borrow.

28.

Teach some kind of class.

29.

Be a student in some kind of class.

30.

Never buy a house without a fireplace.

31.

Once in your life own a convertible.

32. Buy whatever kids are selling on card tables in their front yards.

33.
Treat everyone you meet like you want to be treated.

34.
Learn to identify the music of Chopin,
Mozart, and Beethoven.

35.
Plant a tree on your birthday.

36.
Donate two pints of blood every year.

37.
Make new friends but cherish the old ones.

38.

Keep secrets.

39.

Take lots of snapshots.

40.

Never refuse homemade brownies.

41.

Don't postpone joy.

42.

Write thank-you notes promptly.

43.

Never give up on anybody. Miracles happen every day.

44.

Show respect for teachers.

45.

Show respect for police officers and firefighters.

46.

Show respect for military personnel.

47.

Don't waste time learning the "tricks of the trade."
Instead, learn the trade.

48.

Keep a tight rein on your temper.

49.

Buy vegetables from truck farmers who
advertise with hand-lettered signs.

50.

Put the cap back on the toothpaste.

51.

Take out the garbage without being told.

52.

Avoid overexposure to the sun.

53. Surprise loved ones with little unexpected gifts.

54.

Vote.

55.

Stop blaming others. Take responsibility
for every area of your life.

56.

Never mention being on a diet.

57.

Make the best of bad situations.

58.

Always accept an outstretched hand.

59.
Live so that when your children think of fairness,
caring, and integrity, they think of you.

60.
Admit your mistakes.

61.
Ask someone to pick up your mail and daily paper
when you're out of town. Those are the first two things
potential burglars look for.

62.
Use your wit to amuse, not abuse.

63.

Remember that all news is biased.

64.

Take a photography course.

65.

Let people pull in front of you when you're stopped in traffic.

66.

Support a high school band.

67.

Demand excellence and be willing to pay for it.

68. Be brave.
Even if you're not, pretend to be.
No one can tell the difference.

69.

Whistle.

70.

Hug children after you discipline them.

71.

Learn to make something beautiful with your hands.

72.

Give to charity all the clothes
you haven't worn during the past three years.

73.

Never forget your anniversary.

74.

Eat prunes.

75.

Ride a bike.

76.

Choose a charity in your community and support it
generously with your time and money.

77.

Don't take good health for granted.

78.

When someone wants to hire you,
even if it's for a job you have little interest in,
talk to them. Never close the door on an opportunity
until you've had a chance to hear the offer in person.

79.

Don't mess with drugs,
and don't associate with those who do.

80.

Slow dance.

81.

Avoid sarcastic remarks.

82.

Steer clear of restaurants with strolling musicians.

83.

In business and in family relationships,
remember that the most important thing is trust.

84.

Forget the Joneses.

85. Think big thoughts,
but relish small treasures.

86.
Don't smoke.

87.
Even if you're financially well-to-do,
have your children earn and pay part
of their college tuition.

88.
Even if you're financially well-to-do,
have your children earn and pay for
all their automobile insurance.

89.
Recycle old newspapers, bottles, and cans.

90.
Refill ice cube trays.

91.
Don't let anyone ever see you tipsy.

92.
Never invest more in the stock market
than you can afford to lose.

93.
Choose your life's mate carefully.
From this one decision will come ninety percent of all
your happiness or misery.

94.

Make it a habit to do nice things
for people who'll never find out.

95.

Attend class reunions.

96.

Lend only those books you never care to see again.

97.

Always have something beautiful in sight,
even if it's just a daisy in a jelly glass.

98.
Know how to type.

99.
Never encourage anyone to become a lawyer.

100.
Read the Bill of Rights.

101.
Learn how to read a financial report.

102.
Tell your kids often how terrific they are and
that you trust them.

103. Smile a lot.
It costs nothing and is beyond price.

104.

Take a brisk thirty-minute walk every day.

105.

Treat yourself to a massage on your birthday.

106.

Never cheat.

107.

Use credit cards only for convenience,
never for credit.

108.

When dining with clients or business associates,
never order more than one cocktail or one glass of wine.
If no one else is drinking, don't drink at all.

109.
Know how to drive a stick shift.

110.
Call three friends on Thanksgiving and tell
them how thankful you are for their friendship.

111.
Never use profanity.

112.
Never argue with police officers,
and address them as "officer."

113.
Learn to identify local wildflowers, birds, and trees.

114.
Keep fire extinguishers in your kitchen and car.

115.
Remember that everyone has bad days.

116.
Consider writing a living will.

117.
Install dead bolt locks on outside doors.

118.

Don't buy expensive wine, luggage, or watches.

119.

Put a lot of little marshmallows in your hot chocolate.

120.

Learn CPR.

121.

Resist the temptation to buy a boat.

122.

Stop and read historical roadside markers.

123.

Never intentionally embarrass anyone.

124.

Know how to change a tire.

125.

Read biographies of successful men and women.

126.

Respect your children's privacy.
Knock before entering their rooms.

127.

Wear audacious underwear
under the most solemn business attire.

128.

Remember people's names.

129.

Introduce yourself to the manager where you bank.
It's important that he/she knows you personally.

130.

Learn the capitals of the states.

131.

Visit Washington, D.C., and do the tourist bit.

132. Learn to listen. Opportunity sometimes knocks very softly.

133.

When someone is relating an important event
that's happened to them, don't try to top them
with a story of your own. Let them have the stage.

134.

Don't buy cheap tools.
Craftsman tools from Sears are among the best.

135.

Have crooked teeth straightened.

136.

Have dull-colored teeth whitened.

137.

Keep your watch five minutes fast.

138.

Learn Spanish.
Many Americans speak it as their first language.

139.

Never deprive someone of hope; it might be all they have.

140.

When starting out, don't worry about not having
enough money. Limited funds are a blessing,
not a curse. Nothing encourages creative thinking
in quite the same way.

141.

Give yourself an hour to cool off before responding
to someone who has provoked you.
If it involves something really important,
give yourself overnight.

142.

Pay your bills on time.

143.

Join a slow-pitch softball league.

144.

Take someone bowling.

145.

Keep a flashlight and extra batteries under the bed
and in the glove box of your car.

146.

Take more pictures of people than of places.

147.

Turn off the television at dinnertime.

148.

Learn to handle a pistol and rifle safely.

149. When playing games with children, let them win.

150.

Skip one meal a week and give what you would
have spent to a street person.

151.

Sing in a choir.

152.

Get acquainted with a good lawyer,
accountant, and plumber.

153.

Fly Old Glory on the Fourth of July.

154.

Stand at attention and put your hand over your heart
when singing the national anthem.

155.

Exercise caution the first day you buy a chain saw. You'll be tempted to cut down everything in the neighborhood.

156.

Have a will and tell your next-of-kin where it is.

157.

Strive for excellence, not perfection.

158.

Take time to smell the roses.

159.

Question your prejudices.

160.

Be tough-minded but tenderhearted.

161.

Use seat belts.

162.

Have regular medical and dental checkups.

163.

Keep your desk and work area neat.

164.

Take an overnight train trip and sleep in a Pullman.

165.
Be punctual and insist on it in others.

166.
Don't waste time responding to your critics.

167.
Avoid negative people.

168.
Don't scrimp in order to leave money to your children.

169.
Be original.

170.
Be neat.

171.
Never give up on what you really want to do.
The person with big dreams is more powerful
than one with all the facts.

172.
Be suspicious of all politicians.

173.
Resist telling people how something should be done.
Instead, tell them *what* needs to be done.
They will often surprise you with creative solutions.

174.

Encourage your children to have a part-time job
after the age of sixteen.

175.

Give people a second chance, but not a third.

176.

Read carefully anything that requires your signature.
Remember the big print giveth
and the small print taketh away.

177.

Never take action when you're angry.

178. Be kinder than necessary.

179.
Learn to recognize the inconsequential,
then ignore it.

180.
Be your spouse's best friend.

181.
Do battle against prejudice and discrimination
wherever you find it.

182.
Wear out, don't rust out.

183.
Be romantic.

184.

Let people know what you stand for—
and what you won't stand for.

185.

Don't quit a job until you've lined up another.

186.

Never criticize the person who signs your paycheck.
If you are unhappy with your job, resign.

187.

Be insatiably curious. Ask "why" a lot.

188.

Measure people by the size of their hearts,
not the size of their bank accounts.

189.

Determine the quality of a neighborhood
by the manners of the people living there.

190.

Learn how to fix a leaky faucet and toilet.

191.

Have good posture.
Enter a room with purpose and confidence.

192.

Don't worry that you can't give your kids the best
of everything. Give them *your* very best.

193.

Drink low-fat milk.

194.

Use less salt.

195.

Eat less red meat.

196.

Surprise a new neighbor with one of your favorite
homemade dishes—and include the recipe.

197. Become the most positive and enthusiastic person you know.

198.
Don't forget, a person's greatest emotional need
is to feel appreciated.

199.
Feed a stranger's expired parking meter.

200.
Park at the back of the lot at shopping centers.
The walk is good exercise.

201.
Don't watch violent television shows,
and don't buy the products that sponsor them.

202.
Don't carry a grudge.

203.

Show respect for all living things.

204.

Return borrowed vehicles with the gas tank full.

205.

Choose work that is in harmony with your values.

206.

Loosen up. Relax. Except for rare life-and-death matters,
nothing is as important as it first seems.

207.

Give your best to your employer. It's one of
the best investments you can make.

208.
Swing for the fence.

209.
Attend high school art shows and always buy something.

210.
Observe the speed limit.

211.
Commit yourself to constant self-improvement.

212.
Take your dog to obedience school.
You'll both learn a lot.

213.

Don't allow the phone to interrupt important moments.
It's there for your convenience, not the caller's.

214.

Don't waste time grieving over past mistakes.
Learn from them and move on.

215.

When complimented, a sincere "thank you"
is the only response required.

216.

Don't plan a long evening on a blind date.
A lunch date is perfect. If things don't work out,
both of you have wasted only an hour.

217.
Don't discuss business in elevators.
You never know who may overhear you.

218.
Be a good loser.

219.
Be a good winner.

220.
Never go grocery shopping when you're hungry.
You'll buy too much.

221.
Don't major in minor things.

222.

Think twice before burdening a friend with a secret.

223.

Praise in public.

224.

Criticize in private.

225.

Never tell anyone they look tired or depressed.

226.

When someone hugs you, let them be the first to let go.

227. Spend less time worrying *who's* right, and more time deciding *what's* right.

228.

Resist giving advice concerning matrimony, finances,
or hair styles.

229.

Have impeccable manners.

230.

Never pay for work before it's completed.

231.

Keep good company.

232.

Keep a daily journal.

233.
Keep your promises.

234.
Ask for advice when you need it, but remember that
no one is an expert on your life.

235.
Teach your children the value of money
and the importance of saving.

236.
Be willing to lose a battle in order to win the war.

237.
Don't be deceived by first impressions.

238.
Seek out the good in people.

239.
Don't encourage rude or inattentive service
by tipping the standard amount.

240.
Watch the movie *It's A Wonderful Life* every Christmas.

241.
Respect tradition.

242.
Be cautious about lending money to friends.
You might lose both.

243.

Never waste an opportunity to tell good employees
how much they mean to the company.

244.

Buy a bird feeder and hang it so that you can see it
from your kitchen window.

245.

Drink eight glasses of water every day.

246.

Wave at children on school buses.

247. Never cut what can be untied.

248.
Record your parents' memories of how they met
and their first years of marriage.

249.
Show respect for others' time.
Call whenever you're going to be more than ten minutes
late for an appointment.

250.
Hire people smarter than you.

251.
Learn to show cheerfulness, even when you don't feel like it.

252.

Learn to show enthusiasm, even when you don't feel like it.

253.

Take good care of those you love.

254.

Be modest. A lot was accomplished before you were born.

255.

Keep it simple.

256.

Purchase gas from the neighborhood gas station even if it costs more. Next winter when it's six degrees and your car won't start, you'll be glad they know you.

257.

Don't jaywalk.

258.

Never ask a lawyer or accountant for business advice.
They are trained to find problems, not solutions.

259.

Avoid like the plague any lawsuit.

260.

Every day show your family how much you love them with
your words, with your touch, and with your thoughtfulness.

261.

Take family vacations whether you can afford them or not.
The memories will be priceless.

262.

Don't gossip.

263.

Don't discuss salaries.

264.

Don't nag.

265.

Don't gamble.

266. Lie on your back
and look at the stars.

267.

Beware of the person who has nothing to lose.

268.

When meeting someone for the first time,
resist asking what they do for a living.
Enjoy their company without attaching labels.

269.

Don't leave car keys in the ignition.

270.

Don't whine.

271.

Arrive at work early and stay beyond quitting time.

272.

When facing a difficult task, act as though it is
impossible to fail. If you're going after Moby Dick,
take along the tartar sauce.

273.

Change air conditioner filters every three months.

274.

Remember that overnight success
usually takes about fifteen years.

275.

Fill your gas tank when it falls below one-quarter full.

276.

Cut out complimentary newspaper articles
about people you know and mail the articles to them
with notes of congratulations.

277.

Patronize local merchants even if it costs a bit more.

278.

Don't expect money to bring you happiness.

279.

Never snap your fingers to get someone's attention.
It's rude.

280.

No matter how dire the situation, keep your cool.

281.

When paying cash, ask for a discount.

282.

Find a good tailor.

283. Leave everything a little better than you found it.

284.
Don't use a toothpick in public.

285.
Never underestimate your power to change yourself.

286.
Never overestimate your power to change others.

287.
Practice empathy. Try to see things
from other people's points of view.

288.
Promise big. Deliver big.

289.
Discipline yourself to save money.
It's essential to success.

290.
Get and stay in shape.

291.
If you ask someone to do something for you,
let them do it their way.

292.
Remember the deal's not done until
the check has cleared the bank.

293.

Don't burn bridges. You'll be surprised how many times
you have to cross the same river.

294.

Don't spread yourself too thin.
Learn to say no politely and quickly.

295.

Keep overhead low.

296.

Keep expectations high.

297.

Accept pain and disappointment as part of life.

298.
Remember that a successful marriage
depends on two things: (1) finding the right person and
(2) being the right person.

299.
See problems as opportunities for growth and self-mastery.

300.
Don't believe people when they ask you
to be honest with them.

301.
Don't expect life to be fair.

302.

Become an expert in time management.

303.

Lock your car even if it's parked in your own driveway.

304.

Never go to bed with dirty dishes in the sink.

305.

Compliment the meal when you're
a guest in someone's home.

306.

Learn to handle a handsaw and a hammer.

307.
Make the bed when you're an overnight visitor in someone's home.

308.
Take a nap on Sunday afternoons.

309.
Contribute five percent of your income to charity.

310.
Don't leave a ring in the bathtub.

311.
Don't waste time playing cards.

312. Judge your success by the degree that you're enjoying peace, health, and love.

313.

When tempted to criticize your parents, spouse,
or children, bite your tongue.

314.

Never underestimate the power of love.

315.

Never underestimate the power of forgiveness.

316.

Don't bore people with your problems.
When someone asks you how you feel, say, "Terrific, never
better." When they ask, "How's business?" reply,
"Excellent, and getting better every day."

317.

Learn to disagree without being disagreeable.

318.

Be tactful. Never alienate anyone on purpose.

319.

Hear both sides before judging.

320.

Refrain from envy. It's the source of much unhappiness.

321.

Be courteous to everyone.

322.

Wave to crosswalk patrol guards.

323.

Don't say you don't have enough time. You have exactly
the same number of hours per day that were given to Helen
Keller, Pasteur, Michelangelo, Mother Teresa, Leonardo da
Vinci, Thomas Jefferson, and Albert Einstein.

324.

When there's no time for a full work-out, do push-ups.

325.
Don't delay acting on a good idea.
Chances are someone else has just thought of it, too.
Success comes to the one who acts first.

326.
Be wary of people who tell you how honest they are.

327.
When you arrive at your job in the morning, let the first
thing you say brighten everyone's day.

328.
Seek opportunity, not security. A boat in a harbor is safe,
but in time its bottom will rot out.

329. Live your life as an exclamation, not an explanation.

330.

Install smoke detectors in your home.

331.

Rekindle old friendships.

332.

When traveling, put a card in your wallet with your name,
phone number, the phone number of a friend or close
relative, important medical information, plus the phone
number of the hotel or motel where you're staying.

333.

Remember that winners do what losers don't want to do.

334.

Instead of using the words *if only*,
try substituting the words *next time*.

335.

Instead of using the word *problem*,
try substituting the word *opportunity*.

336.

Every so often push your luck.

337.

Get your next pet from the animal shelter.

338.

Reread your favorite book.

339.
Live your life so that your epitaph could read, "No regrets."

340.
Never walk out on a quarrel with your spouse.

341.
Don't think a higher price always means higher quality.

342.
Don't be fooled. If something sounds too good
to be true, it probably is.

343.
When renting a car for a couple of days,
splurge and get the big Lincoln.

344.
Regarding furniture and clothes: if you think you'll be using
them five years or longer, buy the best you can afford.

345.
Patronize drug stores with soda fountains.

346.
Try everything offered by supermarket food demonstrators.

347.
Be bold and courageous.
When you look back on your life, you'll regret the things
you didn't do more than the ones you did.

348.
Go through all your old photographs.
Select ten and tape them to your kitchen cabinets.
Change them every thirty days.

349.
Own a good dictionary.

350.
Own a good thesaurus.

351.
Evaluate yourself by your own standards, not someone else's.

352.
Remember the three most important things when buying a
home: location, location, location.

353.
Keep valuable papers in a bank lockbox.

354.
Just for fun, attend a small town Fourth of July celebration.

355.
To explain a romantic break-up,
simply say, "It was all my fault."

356. Never waste an opportunity to tell someone you love them.

357.
Be there when people need you.

358.
Let your representatives in Washington know how you feel.
Go to www.house.gov or www.senate.gov
to get their contact information.

359.
Be decisive even if it means you'll sometimes be wrong.

360.
Don't let anyone talk you out of pursuing
what you know to be a great idea.

361.

Be prepared to lose once in a while.

362.

Never eat the last cookie.

363.

Know when to keep silent.

364.

Know when to speak up.

365.

Every day look for some small way to improve your marriage.

366.

Every day look for some small way
to improve the way you do your job.

367.

Learn to eat with chopsticks.

368.

Acquire things the old-fashioned way:
Save for them and pay cash.

369.

Remember no one makes it alone. Have a grateful heart
and be quick to acknowledge those who help you.

370.

Read *Leadership is an Art* by Max DePree (Dell, 1989).

371.

Do business with those who do business with you.

372.

Just to see how it feels, for the next twenty-four hours
refrain from criticizing anybody or anything.

373.

Give your clients your enthusiastic best.

374. Take charge of your attitude.
Don't let someone else
choose it for you.

375.
Work hard to create in your children a good self-image.
It's the most important thing you can do
to insure their success.

376.
Let your children overhear you saying complimentary things
about them to other adults.

377.
Save an evening a week for just you and your spouse.

378.
Carry jumper cables in your car.

379.
Get all repair estimates in writing.

380.
Forget committees. New, noble, world-changing ideas
always come from one person working alone.

381.
Pay attention to the details.

382.
Be a self-starter.

383.
Be loyal.

384.
Understand that happiness is not based on possessions,
power, or prestige, but on relationships with people
you love and respect.

385.
Never give a loved one a gift that suggests
they need improvement.

386.
Compliment even small improvements.

387.
Turn off the tap when brushing your teeth.

388.
Wear expensive shoes and belts, but buy them on sale.

389.

When undecided about what color to paint a room, choose antique white.

390.

Street musicians are a treasure. Stop for a moment and listen; then leave a small donation.

391.

Support equal pay for equal work.

392.

Pay your fair share.

393.

Start meetings on time regardless of who's missing.

394.

Carry stamps in your wallet. You never know when you'll
discover the perfect card for a friend or loved one.

395.

Plant more flowers than you pick.

396.

When faced with a serious health problem,
get at least three medical opinions.

397.

Remain open, flexible, curious.

398.

Never give anyone a fruitcake.

399.

Never get just one kitten. Two are a lot more fun
and no more trouble.

400.

Stay out of nightclubs.

401.

Don't ever watch hot dogs or sausage being made.

402.

Begin each day with your favorite music.

403.

Visit your city's night court on a Saturday night.

404. Focus on making things better,
not bigger.

405.
When attending meetings, sit down front.

406.
Don't be intimidated by doctors and nurses.
Even when you're in the hospital, it's still your body. •

407.
Read hospital bills carefully. It's reported that 89 percent
contain errors—in favor of the hospital.

408.
Every once in a while, take the scenic route.

409.

Don't let your possessions possess you.

410.

Wage war against littering.

411.

Send a lot of Valentine cards. Sign them,
"Someone who thinks you're terrific."

412.

Cut your own firewood.

413.
When you and your spouse have a disagreement, regardless of who's wrong, apologize. Say, "I'm sorry I upset you. Would you forgive me?" These are healing, magical words.

414.
Don't flaunt your success, but don't apologize for it either.

415.
After experiencing inferior service, food, or products, bring it to the attention of the person in charge. Good managers will appreciate knowing.

416.
Be enthusiastic about the success of others.

417.
Don't procrastinate. Do what needs doing
when it needs to be done.

418.
Read to your children.

419.
Sing to your children.

420.
Listen to your children.

421.
Take care of your reputation. It's your most valuable asset.

422. Get your priorities straight.
No one ever said on his death bed,
"Gee, if I'd only spent more time
at the office."

423.

Turn on your headlights when it begins to rain.

424.

Don't tailgate.

425.

Sign and carry your organ donor card.

426.

Don't allow self-pity. The moment this emotion strikes,
do something nice for someone less fortunate than you.

427.

Share the credit.

428.

Don't accept "good enough" as good enough.

429.

Do more than is expected.

430.

Go to a county fair and check out the 4-H Club exhibits.
It will renew your faith in the younger generation.

431.

Select a doctor your own age so that you can
grow old together.

432.

Use club soda as an emergency spot remover.

433.

Improve your performance by improving your attitude.

434.

Have a friend who owns a truck.

435.

At the movies, buy Junior Mints and
sprinkle them on your popcorn.

436.

Make a list of twenty-five things you want to experience
before you die. Carry it in your wallet and refer to it often.

437.

Have some knowledge of three religions
other than your own.

438.

Answer the phone with enthusiasm and energy
in your voice.

439.

Every person that you meet knows something you don't;
learn from them.

440.

Record your parents' laughter.

441.

Buy cars that have air bags.

442.

When meeting someone you don't know well, extend your
hand and give them your name. Never assume they
remember you even if you've met them before.

443.

Do it right the first time.

444.

Laugh a lot. A good sense of humor cures
almost all of life's ills.

445.

Don't undertip the waiter just because the food is bad;
he didn't cook it.

446.

Change your car's oil and filter every three thousand miles
regardless of what the owner's manual recommends.

447.

Conduct family fire drills. Be sure everyone knows
what to do in case the house catches fire.

448.

Don't be afraid to say, "I don't know."

449.

Don't be afraid to say, "I made a mistake."

450.

Don't be afraid to say, "I need help."

451. Never underestimate the power of a kind word or deed.

452.

Don't be afraid to say, "I'm sorry."

453.

Never compromise your integrity.

454.

Keep a note pad and pencil on your bedside table.
Million-dollar ideas sometimes strike at 3 A.M.

455.

Show respect for everyone who works for a living,
regardless of how trivial their job.

456.

Read the *New York Times* and *The Wall Street Journal*
to keep informed.

457.
Send your loved one flowers. Think of a reason later.

458.
Attend your children's athletic contests, plays, and recitals.

459.
When you find a job that's ideal, take it regardless of the pay. If you've got what it takes, your salary will soon reflect your value to the company.

460.
Don't use time or words carelessly. Neither can be retrieved.

461.
Look for opportunities to make people feel important.

462.

Remember that the only dumb question
is the one you wanted to ask but didn't.

463.

When a child falls and skins a knee or elbow, always show
concern; then take the time to "kiss it and make it better."

464.

Be open to new ideas.

465.

Don't miss the magic of the moment
by focusing on what's to come.

466.
When talking to the press, remember
they always have the last word.

467.
Set short-term and long-term goals.

468.
When planning a trip abroad, read about
the places you'll visit before you go.

469.
Don't rain on other people's parades.

470. Don't interrupt.

471.

Stand when greeting a visitor to your office.

472.

Before leaving to meet a flight, call the airline first
to be sure it's on time.

473.

Enjoy real maple syrup.

474.

Don't be rushed into making an important decision.
People will understand if you say, "I'd like a little more time
to think it over. Can I get back to you tomorrow?"

475.

Be prepared. You never get a second chance
to make a good first impression.

476.

Don't expect others to listen to your advice and
ignore your example.

477.

Go the distance. When you accept a task, finish it.

478.

See any detour as an opportunity to experience new things.

479.

Don't insist on running someone else's life.

480.

Respond promptly to R.S.V.P. invitations. If there's a
phone number, call; if not, write a note.

481.

Take a kid to the zoo.

482.

Watch for big problems. They disguise big opportunities.

483.

Get into the habit of putting your wallet or bag in the
same place when entering your home.

484.
Learn a card trick.

485.
Steer clear of restaurants that rotate.

486.
Give people the benefit of the doubt.

487.
Never admit at work that you're tired, angry, or bored.

488.
Decide to get up thirty minutes earlier.
Do this for a year, and you will add seven and one-half days
to your waking world.

489.
Make someone's day by paying the toll
for the person in the car behind you.

490.
Don't make the same mistake twice.

491.
Don't drive on slick tires.

492.
Keep an extra key hidden somewhere on your car
in case you lock yourself out.

493.
Put an insulation blanket around your water heater
to conserve energy.

494.

Save ten percent of what you earn.

495.

Never discuss money with people who
have much more or much less than you.

496.

Never buy a beige car.

497.

Never buy something you don't need
just because it's on sale.

498. Don't be called out on strikes.
Go down swinging.

499.

Question your goals by asking,
"Will this help me become my very best?"

500.

Cherish your children for what they are,
not for what you'd like them to be.

501.

When negotiating your salary, think of what you want;
then ask for ten percent more.

502.

After you've worked hard to get what you want,
take the time to enjoy it.

503.
Be alert for opportunities to show praise and appreciation.

504.
Commit yourself to quality.

505.
Be a leader: Remember the lead sled dog
is the only one with a decent view.

506.
Never underestimate the power of words
to heal and reconcile relationships.

507.
Your mind can only hold one thought at a time.
Make it a positive and constructive one.

508.
Become someone's hero.

509.
Marry only for love.

510.
Count your blessings.

511. Call your mother.

Use this space to add your own little life's instructions.

———◦———

———◦———

Books by H. Jackson Brown, Jr.

A Father's Book of Wisdom

P.S. I Love You

Life's Little Instruction Book™ (volumes I, II, III)

Live and Learn and Pass It On (volumes I, II, and III)

Wit and Wisdom from the Peanut Butter Gang

The Little Book of Christmas Joys (with Rosemary C. Brown and Kathy Peel)

A Hero in Every Heart (with Robyn Spizman)

Life's Little Treasure Books Highlighted in Yellow (with Rochelle Pennington)

On Marriage and Family, On Wisdom, On Joy, On Success,

On Love, On Parenting, Of Christmas Memories, Of Christmas Traditions,

On Hope, On Friendship, On Fathers, On Mothers,

On Things That Really Matter, On Simple Pleasures

Kids' Little Treasure Books

On Happy Families, On What We've Learned . . . So Far

Life's Little Instructions for Wisdom, Success, and Happiness

Life's Little Instructions from the Bible (with Rosemary C. Brown)

Life's Little Instruction Book™ *from Mothers to Daughters* (With Kim Shea)

Life's Little Instruction Book™ *for Incurable Romantics* (with Robyn Spizman)

If you have enjoyed this book
or it has touched your life in some way,
we would love to hear from you.

Please send your comments to:
Hallmark Book Feedback
P.O. Box 419034
Mail Drop 215
Kansas City, MO 64141

Or e-mail us at:
booknotes@hallmark.com